ISBN-10: 149731142X
ISBN-13: 978-1497311428

i

Big and small wonders of Maui.
My favorite photos taken in 2008 while
traveling around this beautiful island.

Thank you to my art and photography coach
Timothy Paul Steward for his
inspirational teachings and for giving me his permission
to print some of his images in this book.

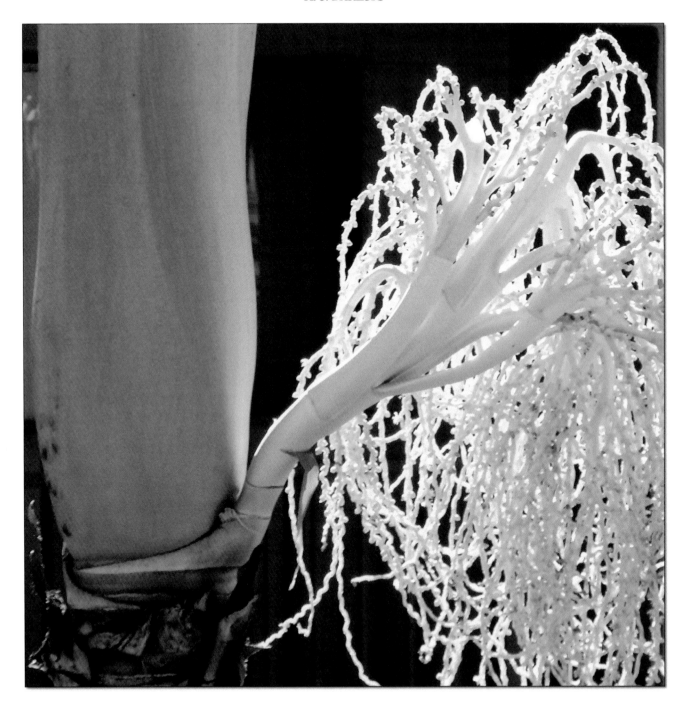

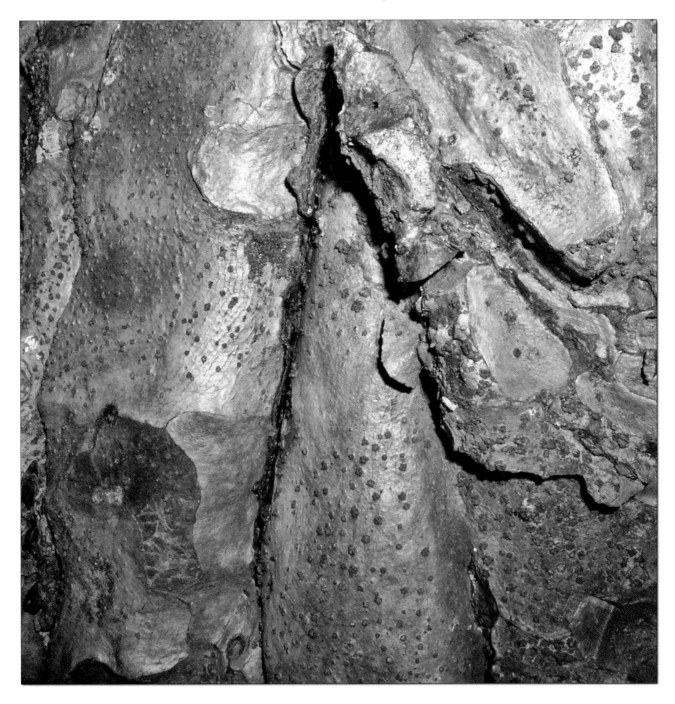